I0471114

How To Interact With Any Kind Of Customer!

Learn to Diversify Your Approach to Customer Service!

By

The Customer Service
Training Institute

Other Customer Service Training Manuals from The Customer Service Training Institute

Customer Service Basics

Conflict Resolution

Service Recovery Skills

How to Interact with All Kinds of Customers

Great Customer Service Over the Phone

Customer Service for Frontline Personnel

Enhancing the Customer Experience

Customer Service Training for Managers & Supervisors

Customer Service Training for Service Technicians

Customer Service Training for the Hospitality Sector

Customer Service Training for Health Care Professionals

Customer Service Excellence for Security Officers

Safety in the Workplace

To our customers because without them,
no business could possibly survive.

Table of Contents

Introduction

Most of us have received training in how to do our jobs. We have been told how to use the office computer system, been trained on company procedures, and usually have received training in our areas of expertise from local colleges, universities, or business schools.

Despite the best technology training or job specific training we have received, one area of training is almost universally omitted. The training that I'm talking about is how to react and interact with the only common ingredient to all occupations and business; our customers.

Our customers are the lifeblood of our existence. Without people to purchase our products or services, we would not be able to remain in business. In order to remain in business, we need to learn how to treat our customers the right way and learn how to keep them coming back again and again to buy our products.

This is not as easy as one might think. Today, competition for customers is more intense than at any other time on our past. In today's marketplace, we not only have to compete against other businesses in our hometown, but we also have to compete with businesses all over the world through the Internet. To make things even harder, our customers are more intelligent now than ever before and have more resources to gain information about all options open to them!

The good news is that many companies don't really place a high value on doing the right thing with their customers. Shortsighted companies manage to the bottom line and make decisions that may save a dollar now but cost them thousands later on. What they don't realize is that good customer service doesn't cost you money. It saves you money!

In the pages ahead we are going to examine what our customers want and what they expect. We will show you how to balance your customer's needs against the needs of your company and show you how to make intelligent decisions that will stand up to the test of time.

We congratulate you on taking the first step towards improving the way you treat your customers. That step alone places you and your company ahead of many others!

What Customers Are & What They Are Not!

While this may seem a little basic to you, we need to talk about what customers are and what they are not. Only by understanding what your customers are and what they represent can you learn to truly appreciate them.

In their most basic form, your customers are people. They are people with the same basic emotions, needs, and desires as you and I. While some may act like it, they are not monsters or beings from another planet! They are people just like you and I. Make every effort to believe this when you interact with them.

Normal people have good days and bad days. Customers do too! When customers are having a bad day, every little thing will set them off and set them off big time!

When customers are having a good day, little things that go wrong and just addressed and handled. The same actions taken by a sales clerk, salesman, technician, or other person may work fine on a good day and just make things worse on a bad day!

Here are some things that customers ARE:

- **Customers ARE regular people**. They are husbands and wives, mothers and fathers, teachers, retail employees, doctors, lawyers, engineers, and every other occupation.
- **Customers ARE people with emotions**. They are people who experience the same range of emotions that we do. They also react to these emotions in much the same way we do.
- **Customers ARE people with real needs**. They do business with you and your company because you address one or more of these needs.
- **Customers ARE people with lives of their own**. They have jobs to go to, bills to pay, and children or relatives to take care of.
- **Customers ARE people with problems of their own**. Everyone has problems throughout their lives and our customers are no different.
- **Customers ARE the reason you and your company are in business**! If you had no one to purchase your products or services, your company would cease to be in business!
- **Customers ARE why you produce the products you produce and do business the way**

you do! Your customers do business with you because you have something the addresses a need and you provide that item to them in an acceptable fashion.

- **Customers ARE diverse.** Just as no two snowflakes are the same, no two customers are the same either. They will vary in age, size, heritage, and skills. Because of this, we must not treat all customers in the same way. To be successful, we must adapt our approach to one that will fit the customer.

We could go on and on for pages listing things that our customers ARE. By reading the above list you should get the idea that our customers are just like us in many respects. By realizing that, we are able to deal more effectively with them on a daily basis.

Now let's take a look at what are customers are NOT:

- **Customer Are NOT people to be tolerated.** Customers are to be appreciated. If you tolerate customers they will feel that you don't really care about them or their needs.
- **Customers are NOT inconveniences.** Customers should never be made to feel that they are interrupting your workday. Remember the last time you waited at a counter while the clerk talked to her friend and made you wait or gave you a rude look? Never view a customer as an inconvenience!
- **Customers are NOT monsters.** While some act that way on occasion, it is usually because they have been lead to the point of frustration by events leading up to that point.

- **Customers are NOT all the same**. They may buy the same product, but their needs may be very different.

Please take a moment to read over these lists two or three times and think about each line item. The more you understand the people you interact with, the easier and more effective it will be to deal with them.

The Golden Rule of Customer Service (& in Life, too!)

There is a fundamental rule when it comes to interacting with others. That rule is: **Treat everyone with respect.** This not only applies to customers but also with co-workers, vendors, contractors, retail people, friends, spouses, and anyone else that you come in contact with.

There will be times when we will disagree with another person. We may even get into an argument or heated disagreement. It is important that we remain respectful of another person's opinion even though it may be totally opposite of our own thoughts.

Remember that every person is different and will have different emotions and viewpoints. This does not mean they are right or you are wrong. All this means is that two people have two different views on a topic or situation.

When we do not treat others with respect, we show them that we do not have any interest in addressing their problems or concerns. We also tell them that their input or ideas are of little value. This causes situations to escalate in severity and inhibits finding a solution to a problem.

How we think of people is shown through our body language. We reveal our feeling by the way we stand, the posture we take, and the tone of our voice when we speak. Our voice may take on a condescending tone, which is extremely annoying to the other person. The other person may not knowingly recognize your body language but their mind will notice it and alter their perceptions, choice of words, and attitude towards you.

When you respect people you tend to proceed with conversation in such a way that it has a positive effect or a calming influence during tense or negative situations. While it is never easy to deal with an angry person, it is much harder for a person to stay angry when they are treated with respect. Most people realize when people care about their viewpoints and problems. When they become aware of this, walls come down and they begin to become part of the solution rather than part of the problem.

Last but not least, some of you reading this will be thinking, "Some of the people I have to deal with do not deserve my respect. They talk down to me, yell at me, and are unreasonable. Why should I be respectful to them?"

That is a valid statement. The way you should approach these people, and the situations they present should be "How can I resolve this matter in the least stressful way for me?" When you look at it this way, you efforts become self-serving and the actions you take will have a real benefit for you. While it may be difficult for you to want to help an annoying and obnoxious individual, you will always be receptive to helping yourself!

Why We Need To Control Situations From The Start!

Human beings tend to adapt their actions to the surroundings they find themselves in. If they find themselves in an awkward or tense situation, they become awkward and tense themselves. If they find themselves being attacked, the will respond accordingly. Because of this, we must realize that the way we treat others has a profound effect on the way they treat us.

There is a common misconception that anger and happiness are purely emotional responses and can be turned on or off at will. This is just not the case. Our emotions are both supported and repressed by physical responses within our bodies. These responses help control our emotions and help us react in appropriate ways when confronted with certain situations.

When we are happy, content, or at ease in a situation our bodies react to this by breathing slower, our blood pressure goes down, and our muscles relax. We become very relaxed and our minds become clearer and more responsive. In this state, we are more able to think and act rationally and have a controlled response to a situation.

When we are angry, upset, or frustrated, exactly the opposite happens. Blood pressure goes up, breathing becomes more shallow and rapid, and our muscles tense up. Our minds become agitated and unfocused. We tend to see and think what we want, not necessarily what is going on around us. In this state, we react more to what we think is going on rather than what is actually happening. We also tend to make more out of a situation that is really there.

These conditions within our bodies can last for minutes or hours after the initial cause has come and gone. Our change of thought or emotion can linger on long after the situation has passed! This is why we have such a hard time calming down someone who is already upset.

The reactions we have to stress, anger, and frustration sometimes get in the way of resolving the problem that caused them in the first place. It is destructive behavior that some people just do not know how to control. These feelings can change the person's entire day just because of one thing that happened in the morning!

For those who don't believe this, think about your own personal life. I'm sure there were many times in your past where something went wrong early in a day and it made the whole day seem wrong. Every situation that didn't go your way just perpetuated this feeling. Each little thing made you angrier and angrier. Finally, when we went home to your spouse or friends, you jumped down their throats about every little thin they did. Everyone has those days. We may choose not to believe it, but we've all had them.

The exact opposite is when you've had very good news, or something has made you very happy. During these days, when something went wrong, you just shrug it off and found a way to make it better. Nothing could get you down; you were the master of the universe that day. You came home happy and, even if there was something at home you didn't like, you just accepted it or changed it. Despite this, you had a good day!

Physical changes play an enormous part in dealing with people. It is crucial that you recognize when someone is in this state and take steps to get them to calm down. Calling a "time out" is very useful if you can find a tactful way of doing it. You can't say, "Hey you look really mad. Why don't you walk around the store until you think you can talk a little calmer." That will just make things ten times worse!

You might try telling a customer, "Let me go talk to my manager" or "Let me see what I can find out" to give both of you a little chance to calm down.

Make sure before taking your little break that you let the customer know you are trying to find a way to resolve their problem and help them out. Hopefully a little break will help resolve the situation.

If you are dealing with someone over the phone that is angry, DO NOT place them on hold. Instead, outline some steps you would like to take to help them and tell them you will call them back in a specific amount of time. This should be as soon as possible, no more than 15 or 20 minutes. (Unless what you need to do actually takes loner.) Then, make sure to call them back within that time frame and proceed with the call.

When we are dealing with angry people, we should first concentrate on getting them back to a calm or "neutral" state. This is the state of mind where two or more people can talk about resolving an issue not concentrating on what caused it. While the causes are important (We should take steps to make sure the causes are addressed so they will not happen again!), our efforts should be focused on resolving the problem not rehashing the cause over and over again!

Personal Baggage

Most customers will come into your store, or call you on the phone with some kind of "personal baggage". We are not talking about suitcases or duffel bags, here. We are talking about needs, emotions, or issues that made the call or visit necessary in the first place. It is important that we identify this "baggage" when dealing with the customer.

For the vast majority of customers, this baggage is the need for a particular product or service. If your car doesn't run right, you come in for a tune up. That is your need and you have come in to address that need. Though the customer is not going to be thrilled about paying for the tune up, there should be no problem in fulfilling this need and creating a happy customer.

This same customer could have the same need, but have much different baggage. Here are a few examples:

1)   The customer needs a tune-up because the last two mechanics did a poor job and now he is coming to you. He will be somewhat frustrated and annoyed because of the time required to resolve the problem and also due to the expense of having poor work done before. He may still be in a neutral state but will probably be a little on the negative said because of past experiences.

2)   The customer needs a tune-up because YOUR shop didn't do the job correctly last time. Depending on how the situation went during the firs visit, and how you handle it now, the customer will be slightly or extremely negative.

3)   The customer is here for a tune-up because the last time he brought it in you didn't get to their car like you promised. Because of the negative experience, your customer will be somewhat negative to start.

4)   The customer is here, because this is the fifth time he has brought the car in and you still have not fixed his car and got it to run properly. In this case, the customer will be in a very negative state and will require extra attention and special treatment.

Here we have the same customer with 4 different situations all revolving around getting a tune-up for his or her car. Same customer, same need, but with greatly different situations and baggage.

How Do You Deal With Personal Baggage?

The single most effective way to deal with emotional baggage is to ask questions and obtain information. Today we have the advantage of having computer systems to hold past history of purchases or services for that customer. Make it standard procedure to always look up past history when dealing with a customer. (I do not suggest this for retail sales. This would cause a huge line at the register or check out line! I do suggest this for any service related business such as auto repair, electronic repair, etc. Past history in these cases can help a technician or mechanic make a more accurate diagnosis or help in determining what the best course of action is.)

Looking up past history can give you insight into what the customer has purchased in the past and what problem he may be having. For example, if he has come in with a problem pertaining to a product he has had problems with in the past; this would be an indicator that this customer requires some special treatment at this time. Saying something like; "This is the fourth time this has been brought in for the same problem. I think we should give you a replacement instead of another repair." This not only addresses the problem but also diffuses the situation immediately and makes the customer felt that you care about his problems.

In cases, where there are repeated problems with the same product, looking up past history can also give you insight into something the customer could be doing wrong which is causing the problem.

In these cases, you could say something like; "This is the fifth time the handle has broken. Most of the time this is due to no fully closing the cover before trying to lock it. This is a common problem so I try to make people aware so they are not inconvenienced any more." This lets the customer know they might be doing something wrong and gave them the information they need to address the problem. Also, note that the person did not say, "You broke the handle 5 times." By not blaming the customer directly, we have saved the relationship between the store and the customer. It's not about being right; It's about keeping the customer.

Later we will go into detail about the importance of getting information and asking questions. For now, just remember that having information about the history of the customer, whether by asking the customer or viewing it on a computer screen is extremely important in knowing how to speak to a customer and properly address their issues.

In the examples previously given about the customer needing a tune-up, you would know how to speak to the customer based on this information. Here are some examples:

For the customer who had work done before at another shop, you could say: "Do you know what they did on the vehicle?

This way we won't be charging you for parts they replaced already and it will give our mechanic an idea of what to check first."

This question let's the customer know that you are trying to help him, save him money, and address the real problem.

For the customer who had to come back because you didn't get to his vehicle the last time, you could say: "Mr. Smith, I know you brought this in last week and we didn't have time to do the work. I am going to make sure your vehicle is next so we can you on your way as soon as possible. I apologize for last time." This assures the customer that there will not be a repeat of last time and that he will have his work done today. Your apology also tells the customer that you care and will go a long way in diffusing any anger.

For the customer who had work done by your shop and the problem remains, you could say: "Mr. Smith, I know you had your car in last week for the same problem. Is it doing the same thing again or are there any changes? I'll assign this to a lead mechanic to make sure that we thoroughly check out the vehicle so you wont have the problem again." This tells the customer that you are taking his request seriously and identifies the steps you are taking to make sure the problem doesn't keep happening again.

One last thought regarding personal baggage. The longer the baggage is allowed to remain, the longer it will take to change it. This is both good and bad.

The good part is that if a customer has purchased a product or service from you ten times with no problems, he is likely to keep on purchasing from you after a problem if you handle it right. No one expects perfection and the vast majority of people understand that people and products are not perfect. As long as the problem is resolved in a satisfactory manner, their feelings for you and your business will remain positive.

The bad part is that once a customer has negative feelings about you or your company, it will take multiple good experiences before the customer will regain a comfort level with you. It may take 5 – 10 future purchases with no problems before you customer starts to feel secure in you and your company. That is why we must focus efforts and resources to identify problems and address them in a proactive manner. The more negative baggage a customer develops, the more effort and resources are required to resolve the problem and keep them as customers.

Creating a Comfort Zone

We have talked about how customers are all different. Different needs, emotions, problems, etc. This is all very true and must be considered when we deal with a customer. Now I would like to shift gears somewhat and talk to you about something that all customers have in common. That is, customers need to feel comfortable doing business with you.

By comfortable we are not talking about having a cushioned seat for your customer to sit on while they wait or coffee and donuts to munch on while they shop. What we are talking about is having your customer feel secure with your products, service, and the experience they have when they come in or call you on the phone.

There are many factors that come into play when a customer makes a decision to buy a product. The main factors are:

Quality
Suitability of the product for their requirements. (Will it do what they need)?
Price
Features
Convenience
Overall value

Most customers do not say, "Today I will go out an d buy a piece of junk that will break before sundown." People want to buy products that are of good quality and have a track record of reliability. Brand names are a prime reason many people buy certain makes and models of product.

People generally buy something because they believe it suits their needs. It is the right size and color. Heavy duty enough for a specific application may be another consideration. For whatever reason, they have looked at several different products and believe that one product is the best for their application.

Price is a determining factor because most people have limited budgets and need to make decisions based on cost. This is why there are a lot more Fords on the road than there are Porsche Turbo Carreras!

Price usually is a factor in two decisions. The first is which product they can afford to buy and the second is where they buy it. They may decide to go to a warehouse club to buy the product because it is cheaper than the same product at a department store.

Features play a role in conjunction with price. Usually there will be a base model and then upgraded models with more features at a higher cost. If a customer decides that these extra features are of use to them, they may consider upgrading to a higher model. On a more basic level, that's why McDonalds has three sizes of value meals. Each one features a different size portion for different appetites!

Convenience also plays a critical role. For a customer to want to purchase a product, it should be easy to obtain and easy to use. By making it easy to purchase a product, you increase its ability to sell. Credit cards make a huge impact in retail and Internet sales because all you do is swipe the card and sign the slip! If a product can be purchased locally and at a good price, it is likely the customer will purchase it in person rather than through the mail. It is in this area that retail outlets can make or break the deal. Ease of purchase is a powerful factor when determining where to purchase.

Overall value is a compilation of everything we just mentioned. It's the "total package". Overall value represents the product itself, where the product can be purchased, and the reputation of the product involved. If everything here adds up favorably, then there is a good chance the customer will purchase the product.

Creating The Best
Customer Experience

Unless you create a product yourself and patent it, it is very likely that you will not be the only source for a particular product or service. If someone wants a washing machine, they can get the same machine at 5 dealers in the county. What each dealer brings to the table for the customer may make the difference in the mind of the customer.

Always keep in mind that people are lazy by nature. No one wakes up in the morning and says' "How can I make things more difficult for me today?" Rather we ask ourselves, "What's the easiest way to do........"

Keeping this fresh on our thoughts, we should realize that people are going to buy things where they have the best experience. The will have the best experience when al the factors we just discussed and brought together in an appealing fashion. Think about some of the real success stories in the last few decades. Each one addresses one or more of these factors. For example:

McDonalds – they provide economical food of known quality in a clean environment in thousands of locations. (quality, price, convenience)

Home Depot – they provide a wealth of products at lower prices throughout the country. (quality, price, convenience, overall)

Warehouse Clubs – they provide name brand products at low prices! (price, quality) What is unique here is that price and quality are such prime motivators that people do not mind standing in long lines to purchase their products!

Restaurant Chains – these chains offer food of known quality at reasonable prices throughout the country. (quality, convenience, price) People like it when they travel and they know what kind of food they will get when in unfamiliar locations. What you get in California you're going to get in Montana too if you go to the same chain!

Virtually all successful businesses depend on one or more of these factors for their success. The one common thread in all of these items is making the experience better for the customer.

We make the experience enjoyable by creating an atmosphere that is enjoyable and comfortable for the customer. A good selection of product, a neat and clean environment, a helpful staff, and good service all contribute to an atmosphere that will make customer want to come back again and again.

Why do you think chains of stores layout every store the same way? It's because they want their customer to feel at home whether they are shopping in New York or Maui! Wherever they are they feel comfortable and secure while in the store.

Selection is important also because to get a customer to come to your store, or call you on the phone, they must feel reasonably sure that you will have what they want. No one will go to 5 different stores trying to find something that they know they can get at a fair price at one particular store. What you want to do is create a feeling in the minds of your customers that they only think of your business when they need something that you sell.

Enjoyable experiences and comfort levels also depend on staffing. You must have the right number of people and the right kind of people to properly service your customers. If you have the right products and the right prices but people have to wait an hour to check out, you are going to lose a lot of sales.

The same is true for expertise. You must have people who know the products and know the procedures of the company. There is nothing more frustrating to a customer than wanting to buy something but they can't because no one can answer that one remaining question.

I encourage everyone reading this book to take a look at their company from a customer's point of view. Look at what the customer experiences from the time he calls or walks in to the time he either purchases or leaves. Break down the experience in small pieces and see if there is anything that can be done to make it more enjoyable for the customer. Maybe coffee and donuts would be a nice step. Maybe it's changing the music in the store or on the phone. There are many little things that can be done at little or no cost to improve your customer experience.

Most businesses don't think about this very much. They agree that it's important and do give it token support but that's about it. Just as in advertising where one word can triple the response in an advertisement, it is possible that one small change in how you do business can drastically improve your sales and customer satisfaction.

Identifying Customer Needs

How to Get Necessary Information From Customers

When you go to the doctor and he asks you what the problem is, do you tell him to guess? When you go to the dentist and he asks you, which tooth hurts, do you tell him to figure it out? I would assume that the answer to both these questions is NO! You realize that doctors and dentists need information from you to make an accurate judgment on what the problem is.

The same holds true for dealing with any kind of customer. A patient in a doctor or dentist office is just one type of customer. That customer is buying a type of service. He or she is either getting a tooth fixed or a medical problem treated.

The only way to do this quickly, accurately, and economically is to involve the individual in the process!

Now that you are impressed that part of your jobs are similar to doctors and dentists (don't ask for a raise!), let's look at why we need information to treat customers properly and effectively.

As we have previously discussed, every customer we have is different in some way from all the others. They have different needs, different problems, and have different backgrounds. Because of this, they are going to require customized approaches. By a customized approach, I mean that we are going to have to get information from them to determine what it is they need.

Sometimes the customer will volunteer the information by just walking up to us, or calling us on the phone, and just asking; "Do you carry Green Giant frozen peas?" This question tells us exactly what the customer needs. In this case, we would either tell them that we do sell that product and show them where it is, or we would say we don't sell that product but we have something similar or better. This is the easiest type of customer to deal with.

Usually we have to ask questions to get the information we require. We need to do this for several reasons. Some of these reasons are:

Customers don't know what information we need – Very often customers will not be aware that we require certain information to get them what they need. For example, if you go into a auto parts store to buy an oil filter, you may not be aware that there are 3 different engines in the make and model car you own. If the customer doesn't know that, they would not necessarily provide that information.

Customers don't realize there are several models with different features – we can't best service a customer when we don't know what application they have in mind for a product. For example, if a customer wants to buy a washing machine, you would need to know how much wash they do each week to determine what size washing machine they need. If the customer has 8 children, they would need the largest size. If it were just a single person living in an apartment, the smallest sized machine would be a good choice.

Customers are not as knowledgeable about certain products as we are- we have the advantage of seeing specification sheets, product introductions, feature & benefit sheets, etc. on the products or services that we sell. We usually know how one brand compares to another and which units have the best reputation or lack of. Customers cannot be expected to have that information and therefore may not know what the best choice is for them.

Customers don't know everything that exists! – We know what's available to address certain needs or problems. A customer may come in to purchase product A not aware that your product B is a much better solution to their problem or need.

There are more reasons we need to ask questions but the ones listed above are the most common.

When we first meet a customer, we want to ask them if we can be of assistance. Since some customers just come in to look around and see what you have, you want them to feel at ease and not bombarded with questions. Asking a customer "Is there something I can help you with?" is always a good way to see if someone really does want help. If they decline your offer, let them roam around the store without any further contact. If you notice they are still there much later, you can ask them again by saying, "I see you're still looking at our .... Do you have any questions I might be able to answer for you?" This allows the customer to ask questions and get information that may help them decide whether or not to purchase.

If a customer does take you up on your offer of assistance, ask them how you can help. Once you find out their need, try and figure out what kind of information you need to know to figure out what they really need.

Before we discuss asking questions any further, I would like to address one very important issue. Asking questions should not be used as an excuse for up-selling customers into higher priced items just to make a bigger sale!

Selling people more than what they need is not a good way to stay in business and build long-term relationships. Use questions and information only to help decide what the customer's needs are and how to properly address them.

When asking customers try to start out with broad questions and then use questions to narrow down the choices until you have a good idea what product will be the best choice for that specific application. Try and think of the process as a funnel. You start out with a large number of choices. As you ask questions, the number of choices decreases until you are left with just one or two options. Here's an example:

Customer: Hello, I would like to by a sound system.

You: I can help you with that. Did you want individual components or a shelf system? (This will eliminate one type of system)

Customer: I don't have much space. I think a shelf system would be best.

You: Great! Do you have a price range in mind? I have systems starting at $50 and going up to $1,000. (This eliminates the real expensive or very inexpensive choices)

Customer: I was thinking of somewhere in the $200 - $300 range.

You: I have several good systems in that range. Do you need CD and cassette decks or just CD? (Finding out which features will be needed)

Customer: I don't need cassette, just CD player will do.

You: Do you have a DVD player? Some of these systems have surround sound so you can get great sound when you watch movies. (Features)

Customer: They do? That's great! The system is going in the TV room and we would love to have surround sound when we play movies. I didn't realize we could get that in a small system! (Customer was unaware but now you've identified an unknown need and made the homeowner happy and excited!)

You: OK! I'm going to show you 3 systems that have everything you need. They all fall within your price range. I really like this one. We've sold a lot of them and have never received any negative comments. It gives you great sound at a great price. (You have narrowed down their choices and made a recommendation to make them feel more secure about their choice.

You can also use the information you received from the questions to make the customer aware of options they might be interested in. For example, we will continue the conversation with this same customer:

You: You stated you use CD's a lot. There is a model above this one that has a CD recorder in it. If you have records or tapes you would like to put on CD, you may find this useful. It's another $35 but you may get a lot of use out of it.

Customer: I do have a lot of old records that I would like to listen to in the car. I could put them all on CD and listen to them wherever I want.

This entire conversation probably will take you 1 or 2 minutes. This is time well spent because of the following reasons:

By taking the time to ask questions, you show the customer you care about their needs.

By selling the customer something they really need and want, you reduce the number of returns and reduce customer dissatisfaction.

Depending on the product involved, a customer might be confronted with over 100 choices to make! By eliminating product that does not meet the needs of the customer, you make it far less intimidating to make a purchase.

By taking guesswork out of the process, you customer is far more likely to buy the product at that time.

Other Ways of Obtaining Information

Some information will be obtained in other methods instead of face to face. Some of these methods might be:

Phone - many times customers will call you on the phone rather than making the trip to the store. Your business may be a phone only contact business such as mail order or a catalog store. In cases like these, you would ask the same questions over the phone that you would in person. The only drawback is you cannot share specific colors or sizes on the phone.

Email- today, just about everyone has an e-mail address. With the growing number of people using the Internet, most companies have some form of Web presence and E-Mail is a common method of communication. E-Mail questioning tends to be slow and in some cases it makes sense to ask for a phone number to continue the questioning process.

Mail – though this is a very form of communication, it is handy I cases where forms need to be filled out and specific information provided in order to design or search for a product.

FAX – home faxes have become more popular in recent years and a lot of information previously done by mail can now be done via fax. There even are automated fax systems where customers can call and request information, directions, etc to be sent direct to their home fax. This type of system is fast and very convenient for both the business and the customer.

Internet (WebPages) – since the Internet is becoming more and more popular, one very effective way of getting information and leads is by having prospective customers fill out forms or surveys on the web site and then downloading the data to you. This is effective because the customers have already indicated their specific interests. Using this information, you can respond using any of these forms of communication. While you will get a lot of just inquiries, this is an effective information gathering technique.

There is no business today that can provide a crystal ball to its employees. The only way to get information is to ask for it in an organized and polite manner. Do not pressure customers into giving you information. Instead, ask for it and explain why the information is important. Most of the time customers will take the time to answer questions if they see a real need for it.

Do not use this information for developing mailing lists or any other income-producing project.

If you have such a need, ask your customer if they would like to participate. If they do, fine, put their name on the list. If they decline, do not place their name on any list. We want to make their experience positive, not induce fear of mass mailings into their minds.

Customers must be made to feel wanted and important. They need to feel that you have an honest desire to help them and appreciate their business. You inspire this kind of attitude by treating them fairly, addressing their needs, and taking care of their problems.

The first step in doing that is by asking questions.

Most Of All, Be Positive!

People react to the words they hear in very specific and predictable ways. For example, the use of negative words will tend to anger or frustrate a customer very quickly. More important, many people will stop listening when they hear the word "no", "can't", or "won't". When this happens, often very positive offers or requests will go totally unheard.

When a person hears the word "no", they almost immediately feel that you or your company has little or no interest in resolving the issue or addressing the issue. Because of this, we want to make sure that we tailor our comments in a very positive manner.

For example, when a customer makes a certain request that you cannot agree to, your don't want to say something like, "I can't do that." Instead, you should say something like; "What I can do is………" . The difference in the two responses is that the first one does not offer anything to the customer while the second one does not say no but instead offers a compromise or alternative for the customer to consider. You may be tempted to combine the two but it is far more effective to approach everything from a positive viewpoint.

It should be pointed out that customers and people in general do not care about company or personal policies that prevent them from getting what they want. Company policies are not the concern of a customer that has a defective product and needs to have it replaced. They also do not want to hear what you can't do for them. What they want to hear is what you can do to resolve the problem or address the issue.

Making a sale or resolving a problem all requires negotiations of some kind. The customer wants this and you offer that. They want A, you offer B. Hopefully you will arrive at a "middle ground" where both you and the customer are satisfied. When this occurs, you close a sale or resolve a problem.

Negotiations do not need to be adversarial. Your approach should not be to "win", your efforts should be on getting something for everyone involved.

The problem with trying to win is that a customer may feel that he was taken advantage of at a later time. The most effective result is when all parties walk away feeling that they got something out of the outcome. When this happens, you stand a much better chance of keeping a customer for the long term.

Substitute any negative words with positive words. Instead of "I can't" use What I can do is". Instead of "That's not" use "This is". Try and direct the conversation towards a positive flow. Here's an example:

Customer: "I know this is 2 years old but it's a piece of junk and I want my money back."

Wrong Answer: "I can't do that because your warranty is no longer valid."

Right Answer: "What I can do is give you a 50% credit towards another unit because your item is out of warranty at this point."

Customer: "I understand that but it never worked right from the beginning. I want a refund."

Wrong Answer: "I can't refund your money. It's against store policy."

Right Answer: "I understand your frustration. I think a 50% discount is fair here because you are out of warranty and with the current sale going on you can get a great deal on a new one. Maybe you would like to try a different manufacturer."

As you can see, the right answers give options and benefits to the customer without giving in to unusual demands. Making someone happy does not mean you have to give them everything they want. What you want to do is give them what they need and what your company feels is appropriate. You may have to give and take a little to achieve a satisfactory result but the outcome may be well worth it.

Make every effort to completely shut down a person's demands. Saying something like; "That's not an option" just brings the conversation to a screeching halt where no one knows who should speak next. Always try to have an option available whenever you have to refuse a request. This gives the customer the feeling that you are making an effort to resolve the issue at hand.

When we talk about demands, we are not just talking about problems. We are also talking about making sales. If someone comes in and says; "I'll give you $300 for that TV" and it has a price tag of $999 on it, you should come back with something like; "I can come down to $750 for that model. If that is too expensive, perhaps you would like this model over here. That I can let you have for $300."

When you handle situations in this manner, you address the issue, provide alternatives, and address the underlying needs of the customer. By providing alternatives, you give the customer options and a direction for the conversation to go. Always remember that we want all situations to be easy to take part in and not stressful for the customer. That means addressing needs and comments while providing options and alternatives. It also means doing this in a clam and positive manner.

Dealing With Angry Customers!

The most difficult customer is the angry customer. The angry customer is someone who comes into your store, calls you on the phone, or sends you an e-mail while they are upset or downright angry.

The angry customer is not the customer who has a problem. Customers who have problems are not necessarily angry. Anger comes when a customer is not treated in the manner they he or she feels is appropriate. As long as the treatment is deemed appropriate in the eyes of the customer, problems can be resolved easily.

It is when the customer feels that they have not been treated properly. This may be true or it may just a perception in the mind of the customer.

Either way, the problem becomes larger as long as this situation is allowed to continue. Generally speaking, the longer it takes to resolve an issue the harder, and more expensive, the solution becomes.

If someone has a defective product, or a problem with a product, and you replace the product immediately, the customer will likely appreciate the good service and remain a customer. They may even become more loyal to you or your company because of the problem! In cases like these, problems actually turn into opportunities!

If you ignore the problem, make excuses, fail to return a call or answer an e-mail, the angrier the customer becomes. In these cases, you may have to refund the price of the product, upgrade to a better model at no cost, or provide additional product or service to make the customer happy. The downside of this is that even though you may satisfy the customer at the end, the customer is not as likely to return as a future customer and will not recommend you to others. The end result is an increased cost to resolve the issue without any long-term benefits. Because of this, you must make every effort to handle problems and their effects as quickly and easily as possible.

Sometimes you may be placed in a situation where someone has failed to do the right thing in the past and the customer now expects you to make up for those mistakes.

When this happens, we again say that the person has emotional baggage. In order to effectively address the situation, we must take care of this baggage.

Getting to a Neutral Position

You can't talk effectively to an angry or upset person. What you need to do is take steps to reduce this anger and get the person as close to a relaxed state as possible. You accomplish this by letting the customer know that you have a sincere desire to help them. Apologize for what has happened in the past if that treatment was wrong. (You may encounter customers who refuse to accept a rational solution or take responsibility for their role in the problem. In these cases, you should not apologize. An apology will do nothing accept validate the customers stance in their minds.)

Speaking to a customer in a calm voice, try and make them understand that you are going to help them. Saying something like; "I see you've had some problems in the past. Let's see what I can do to help you now to resolve the problem." A statement like this is a non-confrontational way to "break the ice" and open up a discussion between you and your customer.

Avoid placing any blame or even alluding to any blame at this point. Even if the customer is 100% wrong, he or she will never admit to it and will get very defensive if accused at this time.

Placing blame on the customer at this time will just make things much, much worse. Make every effort to be non-confrontational during this part of the conversation.

Your goal at this time should be to relive the customer's anger and frustration and get them to a point where they do not feel upset or angry. They do not have to feel happy, either. They just need to feel neutral at this point.

Feeling neutral means that you have little or no strong emotions to deal with. People in a neutral state are easier to talk to and obtain meaningful information. It is almost impossible for angry or upset people to hold a rational conversation and provide accurate and useful information. Emotions cloud the customer's mind and tend to muddle their thought process.

Some suggestions for easing tension and helping customers get to a neutral state:

Offer a calming statement indicating you are willing and eager to help.

Use positive words in your conversation. Use can and will instead of can't and won't.
Speak in a calm and soft voice

Concentrate on what you can do. Customers do not care about things you can't do. Customers also do not care about policies or rules that may get in the way of resolving their problems.

Offer a customer a cup of water or coffee. Sometimes a little break can be useful to reduce anger and frustration.

Don't get too close to the person you are talking to. This will tend to make the other person feel uneasy or threatened.

Smile and act friendly. Be aware of your body language. Try and keep your stance open and do not cross your arms or act defensive. This will make it easier to calm down a customer.

Do not rush the customer when they are talking about their problem. Letting a customer "vent" is very effective is reducing frustrations. Cutting off a customer will give the impression that you are not interested in what they have to say.

If you are successful in calming own the customer, you can use the information gathering techniques discussed in the previous chapter to get the correct information to resolve the problem.

If you can't calm down the customer, you may need to make a decision on how to proceed. When confronted by a customer that you can't help or calm down, you have the following options:

Get another person to work with this customer. This may be a manager who has more authority or a person in another department or maybe even another company.

Direct the customer to their next step required to resolve the problem. In these cases, it may be possible that the customer is asking you to do something that may not be your responsibility.

When this occurs, you should inform the customer of what they have to do next and provide them the information (name, address, phone number, etc.) to help them proceed. Continue to work with the customer towards resolving the problem.

Getting someone else to help is usually used when the customer is not happy with your answers or asks for something that exceeds your authority. In cases, customers may ask to speak with a manager, supervisor, or anyone higher up in the company than yourself. When this happens, do not take it personally. The customer usually will not have any issues with you as a person, it is just that the customer is not getting the answers or action from you that they feel they are entitled to.

The "passing" of a customer to another person is called an "escalation". An escalation is the act of escalating the situation to the next level. Usually, a company will have an escalation procedure indicating who the next person should be. If your company has an escalation procedure, familiarize yourself with it and use it. If no such policy exists, try and get your company to create one. A clearly defined escalation procedure is an important step in assuring that each customer is treated the same no matter whom they talk to initially.

Escalating a situation should not be viewed as a failure. Rather, it should be viewed as a positive step in satisfying the customer.

Do not let pride get into the way of helping a customer. It is better to concentrate on resolving an issue instead of being "right'.

When You Can't Help A Customer

Sometimes a customer will come to you expecting you to resolve a problem that is not yours to resolve. In these cases, you should make every effort to provide the customer with whatever information you can that will help them.

For example, let's say that a customer purchased a product from your store and it requires service. The customer comes to you to have the product repaired. The customer is not aware that you do not repair the product. You would inform the customer that the manufacturer handles repairs directly and provide them with a phone number or name and address of where the customer would go to get their product repaired.

Another example is when a customer comes in with a product purchased somewhere else and expects you to refund the price or take care of the problem. Maybe the product was purchased by a store that went out of business or the product was purchased through the mail or Internet. In either case, you may or may not be able to help them. In these cases, you should try and help the customer as much as possible.

Another situation you may find yourself in is when a customer demands something that is just not reasonable.

This is usually due to a customer being angry or upset. There are people, however, that will try and get as much as they possibly can out of a situation, no matter how helpful you try to be. In cases like these, you should do as much as you possibly can until you reach the point where you feel you have reached the limit of your authority.

If you feel that the demands are unreasonable you can either refer the customer to a manager or just tell them customer that you cannot help them. The customer then will decide what they want to do at that point.

There are instances where you may want to help a customer even though the problem was not your fault or your responsibility. It may make good business sense to help a customer in the hope of gaining that person as a customer in the future. This may be useful after a store has closed or gone out of business. By helping a person with their problems, you greatly increase the chances of gaining that customers business in the future.

A good rule of thumb would be to help a customer out even if you did not sell the product if the time and costs involved are minimal. In these situations, the possible benefits may outweigh the costs involved in satisfying the customer.

Communication Problems

Even the best efforts, and the best intentions, will be unsuccessful if everyone cannot communicate easily and effectively. When one person cannot understand or hear the other party, it is difficult or impossible to resolve problems.

Communication problems may be encountered when there are different languages being spoken, heavy accents by one or both parties, or the inability of one or more people to hear normal conversations. When this occurs, the frustration level of all parties may increase very quickly.

When Language Is A Problem

In today's society, we must be prepared to deal with many different cultures, races, and languages.

The amount of different languages we encounter will depend on the location and level of diversity in a certain area.

While we cannot be expected to speak every language in the world, a business should be aware of what languages are used in their sales area and be able to provide assistance in those languages. As the population of the area changes, then these needs may need to be adjusted over time.

Perhaps a far more common problem is dealing with English spoken with a heavy accent or broken English. In some cases, it is very difficult to understand someone speaking with a heavy accent, especially if you are conversing over the phone. In person you can use hand gestures, descriptive movements, etc. to help convey your message. Over the phone we are limited to only words and the emotion behind them.

This is not strictly a one-way type of problem. Employees who deal with customer can also speak with heavy accents. This is a far more serious problem in that when the employee is difficult to understand then everyone he or she comes in contact with will have trouble. When it is a customer with the problem, then only the conversations with that person or family are effected.

Because of this, it is recommended that people employed in positions that require direct customer be able to communicate in an easy to understand manner. They should be able to converse with the majority of customers they meet during an average day. This may require speaking more than one language. In some cases where there is a very diverse culture, it may make sense to have more than one individual involved in customer contact. When this is done, each individual can speak different languages so that the majority of customers can be communicated with effectively.

Important Note: *When we talk about hiring the most effective people for a particular position, we are not condoning any type of racial profiling, discrimination, or any act that is illegal or violates any local, state, or federal regulations. All hiring should conform to established guidelines, rules, and procedures. Decisions should not be based on race, creed, or color but rather on an individual's ability to communicate effectively.*

Identifying Effective Communicators

Effective communicators are people that can communicate easily with others. This means that they are easy to understand and have the ability to be able to be understood and also understand others. They should speak the required language and be able to understand someone else speaking that language. They should also be able to act as an "interpreter" between a customer and other individual.

There are many positions that require direct and constant customer contact. It is critical that these positions are staffed with people that are easy to understand and communicate with. Keep in mind that these individuals will be placed in situations where they will be dealing with angry or troubled customers. If they are hard to understand when they speak, frustrations will increase very quickly. People with direct customer contact should be able to be understood with very little effort and also with normal outside distractions such as noise, background movement, etc.

Other Barriers to Effective Communication

There are other barriers to effective communication other than language and accents. Other barriers might include blindness, deafness, mental handicap, certain medical conditions, etc. These situations may require a customized approach.

If there is a barrier that cannot be addressed, it is not out of line to ask the customer if they can bring someone back to the store, or put someone else on the phone, that they can talk to. Very often such an individual can help resolve the situation. This person could be a friend, relative, co-worker, etc. This person can then interpret what the person is saying and help you communicate your thoughts and words to the customer.

When confronted with a communication problem, ask yourself:

Is there anyone who can help you or the customer understand and communicate?

Is there other way to communicate? Sometimes writing down the words can resolve an issue with accents or understanding. Could you use a picture to describe or explain?

As a last resort, could you (and should you) try to resolve the issue without further communication? Sometimes you can get a really good idea of what is needed and you may want to try to help even though you can't communicate well with the customer. Maybe it would entail just replacing a product to address an unknown problem. This could backfire if the customer is the cause of the problem and that cause is not addressed

Sometimes resolving issues requires a little creativity but you will stand a much greater chance of being able to communicate with your customers if you identify your customer base and try to adapt your profile to that of your customers.

Dealing With The Elderly

Depending on your product or service that you sell, you may or may not have a large elderly customer base. If this is the case, you need to address certain factors to help insure proper service to this type of customer.

The elderly often feel more vulnerable and skeptical. There is a very good reason for this. There are a lot of individuals that target the elderly for all kinds of scams. They look at the elderly as a class of people that are not able to defend themselves or protect themselves against fraud.

Elderly people also may feel vulnerable because they no longer can do the things they used to do years ago.

Because of this, they may feel frustrated and upset due to their limitations. Maybe they cannot walk as well as they used to or life as much as they did 10 years ago. These things are not things to be ashamed of but they might be embarrassing to some people. In these cases, a little compassion and assistance will go a long way towards making a person feel a lot better!

Take a look at your operation and see what kind of changes might be able to be made t make your business more "elderly friendly".

Changes could be adding more parking closer to the store, more handicapped parking, or providing some electric "scooter carts" to make getting around your store a lot easier. Perhaps you could waive delivery charges for senior citizens or provide free assembly on certain products. While the value of these kinds of services may seem trivial to you and I, they may be priceless to someone that can't get around well anymore.

Another reason for feeling vulnerable is that there is a huge amount of change going on in the world today and the elderly may feel that they just don't understand things anymore. Their old records have been replaced by something called a "CD". Cassette tapes are now replaced by "MP-3's" To make matters worse, now they are being told; "For more information, please visit us at http://www.website.com." What the heck is that? Internet? What's an Internet?

Something that affects the elderly, and many other groups of customers, is that they have more time on their hands than some working people. Whenever someone has time to think about a problem or issue, the more likely that the person will become more agitated as they think about the problem. By the time they actually get to talking to you about it, they are already frustrated and angry. Think about just sitting and waiting in the doctors office. The longer you are kept waiting, the more agitated you get. Why? Because your thoughts dwell on one thing. When this happens, the human mind tends to magnify what is bothering us until things get blown all out of proportion.

Elderly people may require more patience when dealing with problems. Take the time to explain something to them because the entire concept may seem foreign and daunting. By taking the time to explain, you show good faith and help foster a feeling of security in the minds of your customer.

One of the things that the elderly have in common with every group of people is their need to be accepted and respected. Just because someone is advanced in age does not mean they are any less valuable or any less worthy of your respect. Like any other group, they do not want pity or to be treated in a condescending manner. They just want to be appreciated and respected like anyone else.

It is important to realize that anything that makes a person uneasy may get in the way of making that person a customer. By understanding the different needs of the elderly, we can make it an easier and more comfortable experience for them to do business with you.

Dealing With Younger Customers

At the exact opposite of the customer spectrum lies the very young customer. This is the customer with little or no experience or knowledge or a consumer that is not fully aware of the responsibilities involved in making a purchase.

Many businesses tend to overlook or trivialize the importance of younger customers. This is a big mistake. Keep in mind that the long-term success of your business depends on a steady flow of new customers to replace lost customers. Young people grow up to become adults and purchase adult products and services. By treating younger customers well now, you improve your chances of getting their business when they are older.

It is also a misconception that younger customers don't have much money to spend and therefore are not worth the time and effort involved in serving them. Today, more and more young people are working or have parents that give them significant allowances to spend. Young people buy a lot of merchandise. Depending on what type of product or service you sell, a significant source of revenue might come from this segment o the customer base.

Music stores sell a large amount of product to customers under the age of 18. Hair salons and nail shops do a lot of business with girls starting at 12! To not address this segment of the population could result in losing significant revenue.

Young people require a little more effort in properly serving them. They may or may not be aware of all the different decisions involved in deciding which product is right for them. They may make a decision based solely on appearance of a product. Their thought process is; "It looks cool so I'll get that one". It is your task to make sure that the product is the right one for them.

There is also a tendency by some people to take advantage of a younger consumer. These people are the same people that would take advantage of the elderly. Just because someone is vulnerable does not mean we should tae advantage of them. Keep in mind those younger customers all have parents and grandparents that will realize when their child has been mistreated.

When this happens, they will come back to see you and demand that refunds are made. Now you must resolve the issue and have run the risk of not only alienating the younger customer but his parent or guardian also.

Younger customers may not understand all the details in an advertisement or contract. While it is true that the responsibility lies with the consumer, it is in your best interest to explain the details to the customer so they fully understand what they are getting in to.

It makes little sense to hide anything that will become evident in the future. While this may help you close one sale, the effects of your actions may prevent this customer from doing any business with you in the future. Just like the used car salesman in the movies, your actions will get you results today but your business will not be around tomorrow.

Making any purchase when you're young is new and exciting. Young people are more apt to want to buy something of lower price today instead of waiting and saving their money for something better tomorrow. While this is not your problem or issue, keep in mind that your products and services represent you and you should help your customer make the very best decision possible when they are shopping. Make you recommendations and let the customer make their decision.

Very often a young customer will come in with a parent or guardian when they want to make a large purchase.

When this occurs, avoid the natural urge to address your comments to the adult. The adult is not making the purchase. He or she is just there for support. Instead, address your comments and conversation toward the young person. Answer their questions and interact with them. If the adult has a question, then interact with them but also include the young person in your discussions. The same should be said for the elderly, also.

This accomplishes two very important things. First, it makes the young person feel important and appreciated. This is a feeling that everyone desires. Second, it makes the young person part of the process and you stand a much better chance of getting all the information you need to help them properly.

There are going t be instances where you know you are not going to make any sale to a younger customer. If a 14 year old walks into a car dealership, for example, you know they are not going to buy a car. In cases like these, let the customer roam around and look at your products. Keep an eye on them in case they have other motives but make them feel welcome. The feeling they get today may be a deciding factor when they get older and will be buying their first car.

Younger customers are an important long-term resource for any business. Make every effort to develop this resource by treating your younger customers well and addressing their needs.

Dealing With Professional Customers

Some of our customers will be professional customers that have limited time to shop. These individuals may make $1,000 an hour or more and do not want to spend more time than they have to to make a purchase. Depending on what type of business you are in, you may deem it worthwhile to offer certain service to this segment of your customer base.

I do not mean to infer that these people are more important or valuable to society than the vast majority of us. What I am stating is that they may have special needs that may be worthwhile for you to address.

Many businesses offer special levels of services to those customers who purchase a certain amount of product from them. Airlines, for example, have Gold level lounges, first class clubs, and other benefits for those who travel regularly and pay full price. Clothing stores have private shoppers that assist people make clothing purchases. Even banks offer custom services for large depositors!

If you stop and think about it, a person who makes several hundred hours an hour or even more, can make more money working that extra time instead of doing shopping, banking, or waiting in line. If you spend an hour on line and you make $1,000 an hour, that hour cost you $1,000! You would be ahead of the game if you hired someone to do the shopping for you or paid a higher price to get a custom showing or private salesperson. This is not necessarily about vanity or ego but rather just common business sense.

If you sell high priced goods or services, it may make sense to offer a different level of services catering to this segment of your customer base. In large metropolitan areas there may be enough of this type of customer to make this a very profitable segment of your business. While there will be additional costs involved in providing custom services, these should be more than offset by the higher prices and fees usually associated with custom services.

Services may include a personal shopper, home delivery or shopping, special product purchasing, or any other service that will make shopping more convenient and less time consuming. As long as these services represent a cost effective solution to your customer they will use them and you will earn revenue from them.

One potential trap that should be avoided is that you must not let you service to the rest of your customer base suffer because you start offering customer services. Keep in mind that your long-term success depends on serving all your customers properly and effectively. You should never abandon one group of customers to serve another. The only time you should even consider this is if your company's focus changes and part of that change involves changing your product, service, or customer base. When this occurs, sometimes you need to reconsider your resource deployment and make the required changes to support the new direction.

One of the most desirable traits in successful businesses is the ability to look at a company and accurately determine sources of revenue and new business. Doing the effectively involves looking closely at the available customer base and determining which groups represent viable opportunities. Once that is done, then each opportunity is examined and decisions are made according to potential benefits versus costs involved. Ignoring any one part of the customer base might be the difference between long-term success and failure.

Dealing With Customers With Attitudes!

There will come a time when a customer will walk into your store, or call you on the phone, and this customer will have one heck of an attitude. His attitude may be one of arrogance, superiority, or just have something to prove. Unfortunately, you are the one who will have to deal with them, not the other way around.

It is sometimes very difficult to treat someone with respect when they do not do the same to you. If someone treats you like dirt the most common response is to treat that person the same way. While this may feel good to you personally, it does nothing to make the situation better, it just makes things worse.

It has been said that the customer is always right. This is just not true. The customer may be wrong but the customer is still the customer. The goal here should not be to show anyone who is right but rather to complete sale and gain a customer.

If we go into a situation with the focus of resolving a problem or making a sale, we will tend to focus our efforts on positive behavior instead of reacting to poor behavior. A good attitude tends to direct efforts towards a solution. A negative attitude will tend to direct things in a more negative direction. For the most part, the more negative things become, the more expensive and time consuming the resolution will be.

Attitudes are due to emotional baggage. This means that everything that has happened to a person in the past helps form their current attitude. If the customer has tried to resolve a problem 4 times already with no success, they are likely to feel that they will have no success this time either. Even though you may have a sincere desire to help the customer, they will not feel the same towards you.

We want to try to first calm down a customer by reassuring them that you want to help them. Be understanding and help reinforce this feeling by using positive statements and words. Try not to use any negative commentary or words. Instead, make every effort to use positive comments.

It is also very important that you be understanding but not necessarily apologetic. There will be some cases where the customer's viewpoints or expectations are just not appropriate. Apologizing for things that are not your fault or your responsibility will only validate your customer's thinking in their minds. Also, an apology may be used against you in certain legal situations. An apology may be considered t be an admission of guilt which could come back to haunt you in the future.

Always remember that you should take steps to reduce any attitude that you may come into contact with. People who come to you angry, agitated, or upset will not be able to communicate clearly and effectively. They will tend to hear what they want to hear instead of what is really being said. They may block out parts of conversations that are contrary to what they want to hear. Trying to communicate in this condition is of no use to either party.

If a customer is with another person you may have some success in trying to enlist the aid of the other person to calm an individual down. In cases like these, you need to be very careful because the extra person may actually make things worse if they also have a similar problem.

One effective way of dealing with attitudes is to direct your efforts in getting the person to calm down and then transfer the customer to another individual to further discuss the issue and resolve the problem. One good aspect of this technique is that he original person who has dealt with the angry words and comments (you) is now out of the picture.

Most of the negativity will go with you leaving a customer who is far more willing to communicate in a calm and rational manner with the new person. When using this technique, it is important for you to introduce the person to the customer as someone who can take things to the next level.

You could try saying something like; "I know you have had problems in the past but I'm glad we were able to discuss that. I'm going to introduce you to my supervisor, Mr. Gold. He should be able to resolve this issue for you right now." This provides you with a graceful exit and makes the customer aware of what you are doing and why.

Never take it personally when you are unable to diffuse a customer's anger or frustration. Sometimes it is impossible to undue weeks or months of frustration in a matter of minutes. Your best hope is that you can reduce the effects of previous treatment and minimize the fallout. It is important to realize that the more positive reinforcement a customer may get, the more confident, and less resentful, that person will become. This effort may require several contacts or communications, but the effects will be cumulative.

Dealing With The Knowledgeable Consumer!

One of the most interesting advances in consumer business has been the introduction of the Internet. The Internet brings an entire planet worth of resources into the living room of anyone with a computer and a phone or cable connection.

More and more people today use the Internet for research before they purchase. They research products, features, prices, and countless other information before they even set foot in a retail store! They may even come into your store with more product knowledge than you!

What this means to employees is that they must possess more product knowledge than ever before.

If you try to "steer" someone to the wrong product, or give false information, you are far more likely to get caught today than ever before!

Prices also are subject to instant comparison over the net. With a few mouse clicks, a consumer can get list pricing, compare prices from a multitude of sources, and get the best price for any item at any time! When this happens, the customer comes into a store, or calls a store, and already knows what is a good deal and what is not. Because of this, it is crucial that you always be honest when quoting prices, information, and other details about any product.

To properly interact with a knowledgeable customer, you must be ready and able to discuss all the reasons why they should buy from you rather than the competition. You should point out any value added services that you offer such as priority service, installation, etc. that only your customers are eligible for. In some cases, this may justify an increased price for a product.

A smart customer realizes that it is not just the price of an item but rather the total package that is important. Relying on price alone may give a false representation of value. Purchasing by mail, or over the net, for example, may involve additional costs for shipping. When comparing your competition, make sure you are up to date on the policies of other stores. Do they include all the accessories with the product?

There are many cameral dealers that advertise low prices but they remove items like batteries, lens caps, etc. from the package and charge extra for them. The additional costs make the item more expensive than many customers realize.

Most of the time local customers will buy from a local source if the price is competitive. The reason for this is the feeling of security that one gets from purchasing from a known local store rather than an anonymous mail order or Internet site. When you buy local, you know the store will be there if the product doesn't work when you get home. You know who to contact. You have a face to go with the voice when you purchase. All of these things contribute to the secure feeling a customer likes when they purchase a product or service.

If you are an established merchant or business with a good reputation for quality and customer satisfaction, you will welcome knowledgeable customers. They know your company represents a good value and inspires confidence. They feel secure in spending their money with you.

If you do not have a good reputation or are known to take advantage of customers, then a knowledgeable customer is your worst nightmare. There are many product review sites and chat rooms across the net that provide a forum for people to discuss good and bad experiences.

Any customer that visits these sites will get a good idea of what you and your company represent. That is another good reason that you should strive to treat your customers the very best way you possible can. Once you have a poor reputation, it may be almost impossible to turn it around.

If you are a new company or business, it is important that you make every effort to start of right with Customer Service. Creating a good reputation should be one of your top priorities. Your reputation is what will get you repeat sales and word of mouth advertising is a powerful source of new customers. It sometimes makes good business sense to stand behind problems that may not even be your responsibility. Your efforts should be directed in satisfying a customer not insisting on being right.

Reaching Out To The Electronic Consumer!

There is a huge opportunity on the Internet for just about any business. Having a web presence is crucial for success. There is a growing segment of society that will reach out and search the Internet when thinking about making a purchase. Very often it is the information gained from these searches that determines not only what products are purchased but also where they are purchased. Therefore, a web presence is essential.

Web presence should be a straight-forward and easy to follow experience for the customer. The web site should be well organized and easy to navigate. By easy to navigate we man that a customer should be able to go from page to page easily and be able to find the information they need quickly.

Just like your products change, the content on your web pages should change also. Having fresh content makes people want to come back on a regular basis. A great way to get people to visit your site is to provide some sort of useful information on your site. If you're an electronics retailer, you may want to have a story or column on technical or installation tips, product evaluations, reviews, etc. on your site. This information will bring people to your site and see what your business has to offer.

Most businesses have someone who designs the site and maintains the content. This person is called a Webmaster. The Webmaster designs the page and organizes the content.

You may also want to include links to other relevant information available online. You may include links to manufacturers sites for the products you sell. You may provide links for accessories, service plans, etc. for your customers to consider. You should try to provide as much information as possible on your site and make your site a resource for your customers.

Keep in mind that it is very easy to go from web site to web site on the Internet. Once your customers had to drive from store to store to get information and look at products. Visiting 5 stores may have taken a half-day or even a full day! On the Internet, you can visit 5 sites in just 5 minutes! Also, there are many more opportunities on the net for any product or service you can think of.

You must make sure that your site has content that is better than your competition. Your pricing must be current and your product listing must also be accurate and current. If you list something on your web site and a customer comes in to purchase it, you better have it available!

Do not use the Internet as a way of misleading customers into coming in to your store. Customers value their time very highly and are not likely to purchase any items in the future from companies that use deceptive techniques either in person or on-line.

At the very least, your web site should list store hours, addresses, contact numbers and other information. It should also feature an e-mail address that customers can use to contact you to ask questions. These e-mails should be treated as live contacts and responded to in a timely manner. Some businesses gather the e-mail addresses of those who contact the web site and include them in an electronic mailing list. Be careful dong this as this may be viewed as "Spam" which is illegal. (Spam is the act of sending mass amounts of e-mails to people that have not indicated a desire to receive them. It is illegal to do and should be avoided at all costs.)

There are many services available that will create any type of web presence you may want. From a simple single page site to a highly complex electronic commerce site, you can decide exactly what you want your site to be and they can do it.

Dealing With Customers of Different Cultures

When dealing with people from different cultures, we must take into consideration that beliefs and background of that culture when communicating with them. If we do not do this, we run the risk of offending people or having our comments misunderstood or misinterpreted.

Common differences among cultures may be language, religion, practices, or viewpoints. To be effective, we must know what all these items are and how we will address them. For example, people in some faiths and cultures celebrate the Sabbath starting on sundown Friday. To offer delivery only on Saturdays will make these customers go elsewhere for their purchases.

I strongly suggest that your have some kind of resource available for the cultures within your sales area. This guide should list all aspects of these cultures that will affect they way your company does business with them. It should list preferred methods of interacting with certain cultures that take into consideration all pertinent information. This resource should be required reading for all new employees and be readily available for use as a resource.

Please be advised that you should not develop any policy or plan that discriminates against any person or group of people. You policies should address only effective ways of communication, not ways to discriminate or take advantage of any person.

If there are specific cultures within your sales area, you may wish to contact a representative of that group and talk to them regarding how you can effectively interact with them. Most groups will be highly receptive to such inquiries and will enhance your standing within their community. These representatives can share with you things you should and should not do when interacting with that specific culture. Without this information, you may do something inappropriate without ever being aware of it. Something as simple as touching a person may be misinterpreted or cause uneasiness within your customer. You want to do whatever you possibly can to avoid these situations.

One very powerful reason for taking steps to effectively interact with different cultures is that it can significantly increase your customer base. As you show your desire to respect different cultures, your standing in the community increases and your business grows. Always keep in mind that your efforts should be focused on providing the least stressful experiences for your customers. By taking steps to make them feel appreciated and welcome, you show your customer that you care about them and their needs.

Appearances Can Be Deceiving!

It has been said that looks can be deceiving. This is especially true in business. You may make a snap decision about a new customer that may be totally appropriate and cost you business now and in the future.

Whenever we make a judgment based on appearance, we also alter the way we interact with that person. Judgments based on appearance may cause us to make certain assumptions that may be totally inaccurate. For example, if a person is dressed in a certain way, we may make judgments about how much money he or she has, what kind of purchases they might make, and how we should treat them.

Appearance is dependent upon several things.

One of them is personal choice. A person may feel most comfortable in a sweat suit and sneakers, even if he is gong out looking for a multi-million dollar home. Other people may feel like putting on a suit to go to the local grocery store to pick up a quart of milk! Personal preference is just what makes a certain person feel good physically, mentally, and emotionally.

Another issue might by financial in nature. If a person does not have a lot of money, they may not be able to afford a certain type of clothing and therefore may dress in a different manner than most. Someone making minimum wage, for example, may not be able to afford an expensive suit or a tuxedo to go to a certain social function. This does not mean that this person has anything to be embarrassed about or should feel uneasy. This is just another determining factor.

Physical reasons may also determine one's appearance. Certain physical conditions may dictate a certain type of clothing. Perhaps a person may have a condition that is aggravated by restrictive or tight clothing. This person may then have to wear loose fitting garments instead of a suit or slacks.

Another factor in physical appearance could be the occupation of the individual you are looking at. If this person is a bricklayer by trade, he will likely be dressed in jeans and a t-shirt if he stops to see you right before or after work. He may also be a building contractor that earns over a million dollars a yr! You can't tell by appearance!

In short, there are many different reasons for people to look the way they do. You will short change yourself if you allow yourself to react to personal prejudices and feeling rather then taking the time to make an accurate judgment. Remember we talked about the importance of asking questions, gathering information, and making informed decisions. The same goes for physical appearance.

Let's say you sell expensive cars. A young man comes in dressed in worn shorts and a t-shirt. He looks at some of your vehicles while you and other salesmen are in the office looking at him. If you should fall into the trap of using his appearance as a reflection of how much money he has to spend, you might miss a huge sale!

Who's to say which customers have the resources or are likely candidates to purchase your products? Pass up the guy in torn jeans and you may miss the guy who hit it big on a little known stock and now has millions! Pass up the guy in jeans for the man in the suit and you could miss out on opportunity after opportunity!

Unfortunately, exactly the opposite it true also. Just because someone looks great and dresses in expensive clothes does not mean that this person is going to spend lots of money with your company. In order to know for sure you need to invest time and resources into getting accurate information from this individual.

Many a person has been duped by the appearance of individuals.

Con artists go to great lengths to develop an image intended to create a high level of confidence in the mind of potential victims. These "victims" make assumptions based on appearance only and don't take the time to check out backgrounds and references before investing their hard earned cash! Always get information about someone before you qualify them as a potential customer!

There are going to be instances when you have a real good idea that a customer is just not going to buy from you. A 14-yr old in a car dealership is an example of this. In these cases you must decide how much time and effort you can spend on this individual. Factors helping you decide would be how busy you were at that time, the kind of products you sell, and the overall likelihood of that person purchasing your product.

Keep in mind that most large dollar sales are made after more than one visit to the store or dealer. You never know if that 14 yr. Old was sent to the car dealer to see if they had a certain type of car that his dad was interested in. If you never spoke to the son, you would never know the need of the father! It never hurts to ask a few basic questions and then qualify the customer from those answers.

As for a personal example, I am almost totally bald and I walked into a hair salon / day spa. Talk about someone who looked totally out of place and not a good prospect at all!

A stylist did take the time to talk to me and found out that I was interested in purchasing a day at the spa for my wife! She would end up making a several hundred dollar sale! I don't know if this young lady worked on commission, bit if she did, she made some money just be asking a question.

The point of this last example is that you never will know whom the person that came in to your store is really buying for. It could be a woman buying a present for her husband at the local tool center. It could be the grandparent buying a graduation present for her grandchild or a child buying a present for a parent. In these cases appearance has no relevance whatsoever!

The only way you can tell if a person is really interested in your product is to ask them! If they are interested, then help them. If they are not interested, let them walk around and browse. Just because they are not interested today does not mean they won't have a need for it tomorrow!

Dealing With Service-Related Customers

Service related customers are customers that have a product, or products, that require some kind of maintenance or repair. Addressing their needs requires that you determine the source of their problem, make a judgment on whether the unit should be repaired or serviced, and then assist the customer in making a decision.

Service is a great way to create loyal customers and increase sales! Very often someone will come in for a repair and will then decide to buy a new one instead. If you take care of this customers service needs then you will have a much better chance of getting their future purchases also.

Providing service to your customers will set you apart from vendors that do not service what they sell. Very often, being able to get products serviced where they were bought is a huge factor in deciding where to buy! This is also a great selling feature when convincing your customer to buy. In many cases, providing a service to your customers will allow you to charge a higher price and still get the sale!

Remember, one of the main factors in your customers mind when they are in the position to purchase is the feeling of confidence they have in the product and the store where it is purchased. They want to feel comfortable that their money is being spent wisely and that their problems will be addressed quickly and fairly. Since service is an important consideration, being able to provide that to your customers is important.

Providing service can also help you "steal" a customer from your competition. When a product requires service and the store where it was bought does not provide that service, where do these people go? To YOU, that's who! When these customers come in, show them how well you treat people and they will likely make their next purchase from you instead of your competition,

Always keep in mind that having any product break is a negative experience. To minimize their inconvenience to your customer you should make every effort to complete the repairs as soon as possible. The faster you get the product back in the hands of the customer the better off you will be!

There will be times when you just can't do a repair fast. You may have to order a part or service manuals from the manufacturer. In cases like these, it is important that you keep the customer informed every step of the way. Provide them with an accurate assessment of the wait time based on past performance. Many people make the mistake of promising things that they just can't deliver. This creates false expectations in the mind of your customer and creates problems for you when you can't meet them.

Being honest with customers is one of the building blocks of great customer service. Customers respect honesty and they should demand it. When they get lied to your credibility suffers and you run the risk of losing a customer for life. Reputations that took years to develop can be torn apart by just one bad experience. Do not risk that by promising more than what you can deliver.

If you should come to a situation where it does not pay to have something repaired or serviced, be sure to let the customer know this in advance and be ready to explain how you came to that decision. Do NOT use this tactic to convince someone to buy new just to make a sale. When you do that you run the risk of damaging your credibility.

Some businesses offer trade-ins and discounts for their service customers as an incentive to get them to buy products and accessories.

This can be a very profitable arrangement for all involved. Other sources of revenue include service contracts, preventive maintenance, and assembly of new products.

Keep in mind that service customer represent a very important source of revenue for your company. Their needs are not unlike any other customer. They want their needs addressed quickly and fairly. They want to be treated well and appreciated by those they choose to do business with. Keep this in mind and you will be well on your way to long-term success!

After-Sale Follow-Up

This is the area where we separate the winners from the runners-up! Very often we spend all our efforts into making a sale and then just forget about the customer until he is ready to purchase again! When we do this we lose out on a very important aspect of customer service. That aspect is proper follow-up after the sale has been made.

Follow-up is dependent on what type of business you are involved with. If you sell cars then you should call each customer after they take the car home to make sure everything was all right with the car and to ask if there was anything else they needed assistance with. This would be appropriate. If you work in a supermarket, it would not be appropriate to call each customer and ask them if they liked their can of sliced peaches they just bought.

After sale follow-up can be done via a phone call, survey, or even an exit interview. Phone calls a day or two after purchase are common for large ticket items. Surveys are used sometimes by companies to survey all their customers to get a feeling about how well they are doing. Exit interviews are done right after the sale has been completed as the customer is leaving the store. These are not very common. The advantage of these interviews is instant feedback on your performance. That is why news networks and polltakers do exit interviews during political elections.

After sale follow-up has many advantages to both businesses and their customers. For the business, it makes then aware of potential weaknesses and shortfalls in their systems. For your customers, it reinforces in their minds that you care about their satisfaction and confirms to them that they made the correct decision.

People by nature are prone to second-guessing. Did we do the right thing? Should we have looked around more? Should we have bought the product at dealer A instead of dealer B? All these questions go through our minds when we are not totally comfortable with our decision. These doubts become more powerful as we purchase more expensive items. We don't lose sleep over a $3 cup of coffee but we will have second thoughts about a $30,000 automobile.

After sales support and follow-up create a favorable impression in the mind of customers.

This leads to increased word of mouth advertising, as satisfied customers will tell others about exceptional treatment. This kind of advertising is as good as gold!

Follow-up is only as good as what you do with the data you get from it. If you survey 1,000 customers then do not listen to what they tell you, that is just wasted money! What you need to do is look at all the responses and see if there are certain things that are said over and over in the responses.

For example, if you survey 100 people and 95 of them say that they waited too long to pay for their purchase, then you should take steps to reduce the time frame required for check out. This may entail opening more checkouts or changing procedure to make check out faster.

In contrast, if you see that only 1 person out of 1,000 complained about check out time, that would not be something you should address. While the acceptable percentage is debatable, looking at follow-up data will give you an outside view of what is working and what isn't.

Many companies are surprised that making small changes in their operations can have a huge impact on customer satisfaction. Some things that we never think of can be brought to our attention by these surveys and customer comments. Without this feedback we may never improve our operation or be aware of any shortfalls or problems. In this case, negative comments get us positive results!

One last source of comments could be from a suggestion box. This is not a very good source of data as the number of responses will be lower and only angry customers will tend to take the time to write down a comment and place it in the box. While it is better than nothing at all, it is the least effective method of obtaining feedback.

One key to improving feedback response is to make it as easy as possible to complete the feedback process. This is why phone contact is popular although some may think of it as an inconvenience. If you use phone contact, do not call during dinner or other meal hours, very early, or very late in the day. You want you call to be well received and for people to want to take a minute or so to give you feedback. In order to accomplish this, make contact at a convenient time for the customer.

If you are using a mail survey, consider using a postage paid form or envelop so it doesn't cost anything to provide the feedback. Another option is to have a feedback process that lets the customer give your feedback over the Internet. In this method, you would send a card to the customer, or give him a card when they complete their purchase, that gives a web address where they can leave their feedback. This has an advantage of getting feedback within hours of the purchase.

If you do decide to utilize some form of after sale follow-up be sure to survey all your customers. Do not just give surveys to the happy customers!

Give them to the royal pain in the you-know-what that made you life miserable! Chances are you will meet more of these kind and their comments may help you treat the next one a little better! The larger sample of customers you survey the more valid the response will be. There will always be people who will complain about everything. The price will never be low enough and the service never fast as they would like it. What we are looking for in the results are the comments that come in from several people. Common problems that were experienced in doing business with you. Common praises for a certain aspect of your business.

Also understand that it is perfectly all right to tell a customer that he or she will be getting a survey and that you would appreciate it if they would take a moment to fill it out and return it. Sometimes customers feel that these surveys are more of a promotional gimmick and are not even read by anyone. Let your customers know that you read them and that you appreciate their comments and ideas.

Make the effort to find out what is in the minds of your customers. Take their criticisms and their praise and determine what you can do to improve the experience for your customer. That's the bottom line!

Conclusion

It is important to always remember that all our customers are human beings just like us. They think like us, behave like us, and share many of the same needs and desires as we do. If we remember this, it becomes far easier to deal with them in all kinds of situations.

Always remember to view each situation as a combination of now, then, and the future. That means taking a look at the current solution, what has happened in the pat that is affecting things now, and what you can do to make things better now and in the future.

Customer Service is always thinking about what we can do to make someone happy now and securing their business in the future. If we only concentrate on now we neglect an important part of our business tomorrow. We must make decisions based on both time frames. Get things addressed now in a manner that will insure future business tomorrow.

When you become involved with a customer, spend the time to find out what they need and figure out how you can address those needs. Always strive for a solution that will make both you and the customer happy. Do not try to be the winner. Try and create two winners.

Securing future business means making people happy today. In today's business world, there are many companies that do not make this effort. It is up to you to find out how to do things just a little bit better than you competition. It is up to you to continually look for ways to make the consumer experience the very best and most positive it can be. Your competition will always be looking for ways to take your customers away. Make them work for the business. Don't hand it over to them.

Customers are like gold to a successful business. It costs far more to keep an existing customer rather than going out and getting a new customer. Treat them right, take care of them, address their needs, and you will be on your way to growing a stable and profitable business in the months and years ahead.

For more information on Customer Service Training, please go to:

http://www.customerservicetraininginstitute.com

www.ingramcontent.com/pod-product-compliance
Lightning Source LLC
Chambersburg PA
CBHW072027190526
45166CB00015B/892